THE ROAD TO QUEENDOM

365 Daily Reflections and Affirmations to Keep
YOUR Crown Straight

Queen S. Ofori

To contact the author please reach out to: support@queenofori.com

For my Mother, who exemplifies what it means to be a Queen, 365 days of the year.

For my Father, who taught me the true definition of royalty, through your standards and values, I respect the responsibilities of the crown.

For my family and friends, there's no Queendom without your love and support.

For my Creator, YOU are everything. May all I do glorify your goodness and mercy.

Thank you all.

I love you.

-Queen

INTRODUCTION

It's often said that our minds are like computers, constantly running on "outdated files"—the experiences and environments that shaped us in the past. Most of the thoughts we have today aren't original; they're hand-me-down beliefs and patterns we inherited or absorbed in our formative years.

In a way, we've all been programmed. Crazy, right? But here's the thing: no matter what's been downloaded into our minds, deep within us—especially as women, there's an internal compass, a truth that our soul never forgets.

This truth is our essence, our royalty. And that's what I'll be sharing with you every day in this book.

You see, it's no coincidence that I was named Queen. While that is my legal name, it's also a reflection of something I believe deeply: we are all royalty. Every woman is a Queen by birthright. Whether we realize it or not, we hold the power to rewrite our stories, rewire our minds and reclaim our crowns.

On the Road to Queendom, we get to let go of the old, outdated data that no longer serves us. By deliberately feeding our souls with love, affirmation, and truth, we starve the ego—the voice of fear, doubt, and lies—and replace it with the radiant and sometimes new knowledge of who we really are.

This journey isn't about perfection. It's about embracing our imperfect, yet perfect, selves. It's about creating heaven on earth in our everyday lives, whether as mothers, sisters, daughters, friends, or leaders. Life doesn't have to be hard. It gets to be beautiful, joyful, surprising, and full of love—if we allow it.

My hope is that this book becomes your daily guide and gentle reminder of your birthright as a Queen.

May these affirmations and reflections help you rediscover the truth of who you are and replace the files of doubt and fear with confidence and clarity.

May you feel your crown firmly on your head 365 days of the year. And on the days when your crown feels heavy, may these words lift you up, straighten your posture, and remind you of your strength and sovereignty.

Together, let's journey toward the truth, healing, and transformation. Let's embark on the Road to Queendom.

JANUARY

01
JANUARY

You are love. You are special. You are important.
You are worthy of good things.
Accept this as truth, Queen.

Reflection

What would it take for you to believe the statements
above and if you already have this mindset, how can
we turn it up a notch?

02
JANUARY

Queen, ensure that your behavior <u>consistently</u> reflects the dynamic and radiant person you claim to be (even on the days it feels most challenging).

Reflection

If no words were spoken and people could only judge you by your actions, what would they say?

03

JANUARY

In life, there are no losses, just learning lessons.

Look for the lesson, Queen.

Reflection

What's something you learned the hard way?

04
JANUARY

Dear Queen, you are and will forever be
the best part of life.

Anything and anyone would be lucky to have you.

Reflection

Does your outer world reflect your inner truth?
What's one thing you can do today to get in
alignment?

05

JANUARY

Progress over perfection.

As long as you're doing your best, it is enough, Queen.

Reflection

Have you been giving your all to your endeavors?
Can you surrender to the outcome
(whether it's perfect or not)?

06
JANUARY

Queen, as Confucius once said, "wherever you go today, go with your whole heart."

Reflection

Are you living a passionate life?
If not, what are you waiting for?

07
JANUARY

In all interactions today: make eye contact, place your shoulders back and keep your head held high.
You are a QUEEN.
Act like it.

Reflection

Where is your confidence level? Write a list of what you can do to increase your esteem. And if you're already at a level 10, remember: 11 is always available.

08

JANUARY

It's not what people say and call you that matters, Queen.

It's what and who you answer to.

Reflection

What are you choosing to respond to today?

09
JANUARY

Surrender, Queen.
Even when you don't understand.
Trust that a bigger plan is unfolding for your life.

Reflection

What are you gaining when you worry?
What could you gain by letting go?

10
JANUARY

Less judgement.
More grace, Queen.

Reflection

How can you gift yourself more kindness today?

11
JANUARY

Happiness is a choice.

Choose it as often as possible, Queen.

Reflection

What's one thing you can do today to add a smile to your face?

12
JANUARY

Take a moment to appreciate yourself.
Despite every challenge, your resilience never
wavered, Queen.

What's more majestic than that?

Reflection

Think of all the times you showed up for you.
Write yourself a "thank you" letter today.

13
JANUARY

In your heart, you're aware of your path.
You know the steps to take and the timing for the
appropriate action.
Get still. Get grounded.
And get moving, Queen.

Reflection

Are your priorities in order?

14
JANUARY

You are the blessing someone is waiting on, Queen.

Don't forget that.

Reflection

Do you recognize the good you bring into the world?

15

JANUARY

If you want love, be loving.
If you want joy, be joyful.
If you want more money, give more money.

When life seems to stand still,
share the very thing you think is missing, Queen.

Reflection

How will you be of service today?

16
JANUARY

Make a list of three things you are grateful for.

Meditate on this list all day, Queen.

Reflection

How can you stay in a space of gratitude more often?

17
JANUARY

I'm so, so, very proud of you, Queen.

Reflection

Place your right hand over your heart and repeat this
five times (out loud):

"I acknowledge your effort, Queen."

18

JANUARY

Life is always speaking to you.

Get present & pay attention to the signs, Queen.

Reflection

What's been on your heart lately?

19

JANUARY

Your career, relationships, finances and health will
always be a reflection of what you believe about yourself.

If you want the best, you must decide YOU are the best.

Work diligently to maintain
a high level of esteem, Queen.

Reflection

What's one thing you can do to increase your level
of confidence?

20

JANUARY

Be loving today. Be fun. Be joyous. Be silly.
Be honest about what you want.
Be magical, Queen.

Reflection

What does it feel like to rest in your feminine
energy? How does it feel to just "be"?

21
JANUARY

Every blessing assigned to you is coming, Queen.

Know and affirm this daily.

Reflection

What empowering truth are you choosing to embrace today?

22

JANUARY

In all your commitments, focus on your strengths.
Know them like the back of your hand
and use them as leverage, Queen.

Reflection

What are five things you naturally excel at?

Write them down and consider how you can
maximize on them.

23

JANUARY

However it goes, you will win in the end, Queen.

So, if you haven't won yet, it's not the end.

Reflection

What would "winning" in this season of your
life look like for you?

24

JANUARY

You are not "too much" for the right person, Queen.

Choose your tribe wisely.

Reflection

Do you ever feel like you have to shrink?
During those times, who or what are you around?

25
JANUARY

Self-awareness, Queen.
Practice self-awareness today.

Reflection

What can you do to get to know yourself better?

26

JANUARY

Protect your dreams at all costs, Queen.

Reflection

Would you be willing to keep some goals to yourself
and let the results do the talking?

27

JANUARY

Psalm 126:5, Queen.

Reflection

Are you ready for your blessings?

28

JANUARY

There is a gift in rejection.
There is also a gift in redirection.
Count it all as joy, Queen.

Reflection

What's one good thing that has come from a
negative moment?

29

JANUARY

Make sure you use the power
of your "yes" wisely today, Queen.

Reflection

What are you <u>choosing</u> and is it what you really
want?

30

JANUARY

Remember Queen, when someone walks away from you, they are doing you a favor.

There is good in goodbye.

Reflection

Are you honoring and celebrating the necessary endings in your life?

31
JANUARY

You already have everything you need
to move forward, Queen.

No more waiting.

It's time to make a move.

Reflection

Do you know how much of a boss you are?

FEBRUARY

01

FEBRUARY

Queen, you are not alone in your journey of life.
Countless women have paved the way for you, and
countless more will follow in your footsteps.
Make your choices count.

Reflection

How do you want to be remembered?
What will be your legacy?

02
FEBRUARY

We are always in the process of evolving.
Yet, who we are at the core will always remain.

At the core,
you are light.
You are love.
You are good, Queen.

Never forget this.

Reflection

What can you do every day to get grounded in the
truth of who you are?

03

FEBRUARY

God has your back, Queen and God won't fail you.

Reflection

What are you trusting God for today?
Take a moment to write it down.

04

FEBRUARY

<u>You</u> are who you've been waiting on, Queen.

<u>You</u> are the one who will give yourself
the life of your dreams.

Reflection

How can you use your mind to create opportunities
for success?

05

FEBRUARY

Take a new road. Wear a bold color.
Style your hair a different way.
Do something new, Queen.

Reflection

What excitement can you spark today?

06
FEBRUARY

You become confident through action, Queen.

Not talking about what you're planning to do.

Reflection

What are your actions saying about who you are?

07

FEBRUARY

When you are in alignment with what's for you,
there will be less questions and more answers, Queen.

Reflection

Are you at peace with the people, places and things
in your life?

08

FEBRUARY

Everything is conspiring in your favor, Queen.

Reflection

Do you know (like really know) how special you are?

09

FEBRUARY

Just for today, release the need to worry, Queen.

Use all your energy to believe.

Reflection

Can you train your mind to think positively for the next 24 hours?

10
FEBRUARY

Divine timing, Queen.

Everything will occur for you in divine timing.

Reflection

Are you willing to trust that things are working out the way they are supposed to, even when you don't understand?

11
FEBRUARY

Gift yourself flowers, Queen.
Despite what the world may say, you are doing an
amazing job and you make it look easy.
Be proud of that.

Be proud of you.

Reflection

Are you giving yourself enough credit for all the
things you've created in your life (big and small)?

12
FEBRUARY

Trust life and flow today, Queen.

Trust and flow.

Reflection

Do you always have to be in control?
Where does this need stem from?

13

FEBRUARY

Remember, someone having a different perspective,
personality or approach toward things
doesn't make them wrong, Queen.

Reflection

How do you deal with people who think differently
from you?

14
FEBRUARY

Practice vulnerability today, Queen
(no matter how hard it gets).

Repeat: I will be courageous. I will be honest.

Reflection

Can you commit to being uncomfortable?

15
FEBRUARY

Hope is not a strategy, Queen.

Create tactics and pair them with good intentions for your success.

Reflection

Do you feel confident in achieving your goals?

16
FEBRUARY

Make loving yourself a habit, Queen.

Reflection

When's the last time you said "I love you" to you?

17
FEBRUARY

Teach people the rules of your Queendom by setting unapologetic boundaries, Queen.

Teach people how to treat you.

Reflection

How do you share your boundaries with others and what do you do when someone crosses it?

18
FEBRUARY

Inhale and hold for four seconds.
Exhale and hold for four seconds.
Deep breaths today, Queen.

Deep breaths.

Reflection

How does it feel to be alive?

19
FEBRUARY

Create the plan, Queen.
Don't worry about the how.
Focus on who you need to BE to make things happen.
Then, work on becoming.

Reflection

In your journal, describe the attributes of the most
powerful version of yourself. What does she wear?
Where does she go? What does she do all day?

20
FEBRUARY

Give away something old today.
Whether it's an article of clothing, a relationship or mindset.

Let go of what is no longer serving you, Queen.

Reflection

What will you release today?

21
FEBRUARY

If there is an honorable man in your life that has been good to you: a father, brother, husband, teacher, uncle or friend, show gratitude today.

Say thank you, Queen.

Reflection

How do you define a "good man" and what are the origins of your definition?

22
FEBRUARY

Eat slowly, Queen.
Laugh fully, until your belly hurts.
Cry with all your heart.
Give everything you do, all you've got.
Then, watch how your Queendom transforms.

Reflection

How would it feel to live life at 100%?

23

FEBRUARY

If it's easier to leave, stay.
Don't jump to do what's easy, Queen.
Strive to do what's best.

Reflection

What is your "go-to" habit when avoiding a
challenge?

24
FEBRUARY

Begin with the end in mind, Queen.

Reflection

What do you do to set the desired tone in new
situations?

25
FEBRUARY

Prayer works, Queen.
Try it.

Reflection

What is your prayer life looking like?

26
FEBRUARY

Don't forget, Queen: you are entitled to miracles.

Reflection

What's one miracle you are expecting today?
Meditate on it.

27

FEBRUARY

Your blessings are on the way, Queen.

Are you ready?

Reflection

How are you preparing for what you want?

28
FEBRUARY

Your body is a holy temple, Queen.

Cherish it.

Cherish you.

Reflection

Have you been honoring your body?

29
FEBRUARY

Failure is a myth, Queen.
There's valuable feedback and lessons to be learned
from every setback.
Embrace the learning, pause to recommit and then,
continue moving forward.

Reflection

What would you do if you knew you couldn't fail?

MARCH

01
MARCH

Queen, <u>choose</u> abundance over scarcity.
<u>Select</u> growth mindset over fixed mindset.
<u>Prefer</u> urgency over desperation.

Reflection

What type of energy will you show up with today?

02
MARCH

The universe is in love with you, Queen
and there's nothing you can do about it.

Reflection

In your journal or with a trusted friend, sincerely
acknowledge the love that is already present in your
life.

03
MARCH

Simplicity, Queen.

Keep things simple today.

Reflection

What's on your "to-do" list that shouldn't be?

04
MARCH

Everyone makes mistakes, Queen.

Give yourself permission to be human.

Reflection

How can you give yourself more grace today?

05
MARCH

Forgiveness.

Forgiveness will set you free, Queen.

Reflection

Who might you release from blame?
How will you do it?

06
MARCH

Do something to put a smile on your face today,
Queen.

Reflection

What lights you up?

07
MARCH

Gratitude, Queen.

Practice gratitude.

Reflection

What is one thing you can be grateful for today?

08
MARCH

Queen, at the end of each day write down:

1. Three things that worked for you.
2. Three things that didn't work for you.
3. Three things you will do differently moving forward.

Reflection

What is your empowering night routine?
Can you commit to starting one?

09
MARCH

You are a sweet and kind soul, Queen.
You are not your actions or feelings.
Don't ever forget that.

Reflection

Can you make peace with the decisions and
statements made when you weren't feeling your best?

10
MARCH

Embrace yourself to be embraced by others, Queen.

Be a friend to you first.

Reflection

What is your definition of <u>self</u>-love?

11
MARCH

We all desire connection.
However, we must weigh the opportunity costs.
Make sure you aren't losing when trying to gain what
you really want, Queen.

Reflection

Have you ever felt like you had to betray yourself?
What steps can you take to avoid feeling that way
ever again?

12
MARCH

Do what you love, Queen.

Life is too precious to do anything else.

Reflection

What makes your heart sing?
Can you do it more often?

13
MARCH

Write a personal encouragement note for yourself
and keep it in a sacred place.
Whenever you seek a boost of confidence,
turn to this note.

Embrace your inner strength, Queen.

Reflection

What's your favorite affirmation during tough times?

14
MARCH

Kindness, Queen.

Mindfully, practice kindness today.

Reflection

Can you think of someone exceptionally kind
in your life?

15
MARCH

Maintain relationships with people who love you even on the hard days, Queen.

(Not only when it's convenient.)

Reflection

Who or what comes to mind when you think of unconditional love?

16
MARCH

Moving forward, replace the phrase "I can't" with "how can I?"

Then, observe the new possibilities that come forth, Queen.

Reflection

Which opportunities have you written off as "impossible"? Why?

17
MARCH

Talk less.

Listen more, Queen.

Reflection

Have you been listening or just waiting to respond?

18
MARCH

When you feel sad or lost, create a plan.
Base your outline on how you want to feel.
Allow this clear vision to <u>move</u> you forward, Queen.

Reflection

What do you want your life to feel like?
What's your vision?

19
MARCH

BIG people talk and focus on BIG things.
Little people talk and focus on little things.
Which one are you, Queen?

Reflection

What are your day-to-day conversations normally
about?

20
MARCH

Even when things get hard,
make a decision to persevere, Queen.

Reflection

What type of day have you decided to have?

21
MARCH

Take things one minute at a time, Queen.

Sometimes, one second at a time.

Reflection

How can you lighten your load today?

22
MARCH

Your path doesn't have to look the same as everyone else's, Queen.

Your life. Your conditions.

Reflection

How does it feel to create your own rules?

23
MARCH

Destiny over distractions, Queen.

Reflection

Always question if what you're dealing with is
furthering your purpose or taking you farther away
from it?

24
MARCH

You are one thought, one conversation & one mindset
shift away from an entirely different life, Queen.
Just one.

Don't give up.

Reflection

How can you energize yourself on your road to
Queendom?

25
MARCH

It's important to seek out a mentor who inspires you,
and equally important to become a mentor, imparting
wisdom and guidance to others, Queen.

Reflection

What qualities make a great mentor?

26
MARCH

Faith and doubt are both aspects of belief, Queen.

Reflection

What are you choosing to believe in?

27
MARCH

You never know what unspoken battles people are facing, Queen.

Practice radical kindness today.

Reflection

Recall a time someone was nice to you, especially when you needed it most.

Be that person for someone else today.

28
MARCH

Pay attention to actions, Queen.

Actions (not words) will give you all the information
you need.

Reflection

Are the actions of those around you
consistent with their words?

29
MARCH

Speak your truth, Queen.
(Even if your voice trembles.)

Reflection

How will you push through when it's time to speak
up?

30
MARCH

Whenever you find yourself feeling nervous, confused, or anxious, take a moment to reflect.

Observe your actions and consider the thoughts that are driving them, Queen.

Reflection

Why do you do the things you do?

31
MARCH

Capacity is a state of mind, Queen.

You can handle a lot more than you think you can.

Reflection

Why stop at good, when you can be great?

APRIL

01
APRIL

You are qualified, Queen.
Walk like it and talk like it.
Embrace this season with confidence and grace,
knowing that all good things are rightfully yours.

Reflection

What are three of your most outstanding
qualifications?

02
APRIL

Don't compare, Queen.

The beauty you see in others is a reflection of you.

Reflection

Do you feel secure in your skin?

03
APRIL

Affirm yourself every day, through your words and actions.

Think highly of yourself, Queen.

Reflection

How do you view yourself?

04
APRIL

You are blessed and highly favored, Queen.
You are God's favorite.
Ingrain this deeply.
Move accordingly.

Reflection

How divine are you?

05
APRIL

Do not take anything personal, Queen.
The words and thoughts of others are often a mirror
of their own reality.

Reflection

How can you stop yourself from absorbing people's
negative energy?

06
APRIL

Today, do what's best for you, Queen.
Offer no explanations whatsoever.
<u>None</u>.

Reflection

Do you think explanations are always mandatory?
Where did you learn this?

07
APRIL

Choices + speech = confidence, Queen.

Reflection

Write about your current self-esteem.
Is it where you want it to be or is it hindering you?

08
APRIL

It's essential to nurture oneself before giving to others, Queen.

Make sure to fill your cup up first.

Reflection

What can you do or refrain from doing to recharge yourself today?

09

APRIL

Begin before you "feel" like it.
Start new habits, Queen and your feelings will catch
up.

Reflection

What is a single action you can initiate now that will
propel you towards the achievement of your goals?

10
APRIL

Don't let the past rob you of the present, Queen.
Who you were yesterday does not have to define you.
You can create a new story.
You can choose a new path.

Reflection

Do you realize you have the power to choose?

11
APRIL

Your mind is one of your greatest assets, Queen.

The job, clothes, cars and money are just a byproduct.

Reflection

Are you aware of just how brilliant you are?

12
APRIL

If you have ever achieved success, rest assured, you have the power to do it again and again, Queen.

Reflection

What are your top three accomplishments?

13
APRIL

People may try to imitate you, but <u>YOU</u> are the magic.

You are irreplaceable, Queen, and that is your power.

Reflection

List three things that make you unique.

14
APRIL

You are a big deal, Queen.
Don't ever play about you.
And never let anyone else play about you either.

Reflection

Are you ready to get serious about you?

15
APRIL

Queen's motto: no negativity allowed.

Reflection

What can you do in advance to maintain a positive
outlook throughout the day?

16
APRIL

Honor your existence and the worth you carry,
Queen.

Be conscious of how and with whom you spend your
time.

Reflection

Are you preserving your energy for the things that
matter?

17
APRIL

Be open to connecting with individuals beyond your immediate circle.

Growth and success often stem from engaging with a diverse group of people, not just those who look like you, Queen.

Reflection

Is there diversity in your network?

18
APRIL

The sorrows, setbacks, deceptions, and denials you've experienced were ultimately for your benefit, Queen.

Affirm: "Everything <u>always</u> works out for my good."

Reflection

How can you help someone else to heal with the wisdom gained from your lessons?

19
APRIL

There is a little girl inside of you, seeking your unwavering protection, love, and appreciation.

Keep her safe, Queen.

Reflection

How old is your inner child?
What does she like to do?

20

APRIL

You have to be a good friend
to have and <u>keep</u> a good friend, Queen.

Reflection

On a scale from 1 to 10, (10 being great) how would
you rate the quality of your friendships?

21
APRIL

Drop anything that is unhealthy, Queen.
Consume nourishment that benefits your well-being.
When you eat better, you look and feel better.

Reflection

What's one thing you can add or remove from your
diet, that would make all the difference?
Can you implement this change for one week?

22
APRIL

You are the only one responsible for your life, Queen.

YOU.

Reflection

What action(s) can you take in this moment to make sure you're okay?

23
APRIL

You are right on schedule, Queen.

Trust the timing of your life.

Reflection

What's your relationship with trust like?

24
APRIL

You can choose to enhance your appearance if you like, Queen.

Just remember, the innate beauty you possess will always radiate the most.

Reflection

How do you feel about your natural features?

25
APRIL

On the road to Queendom, rest if you must.

Cry. Pause. Reflect.

Just never give up, Queen.

Reflection

What do you need to do to restore focus?

26
APRIL

Hold yourself in high regard, Queen.

You are a very important person.

All day repeat: "I'm a VIP" and notice the shift
in your presence.

Reflection

Do you know how important you are?

27
APRIL

True self-worth is something only YOU can give to yourself, Queen.

No one else's validation will ever make up for it.

Reflection

How has your self-esteem been playing a role in what you accept in life?

28
APRIL

Weeping may endure for a night, but joy comes in the morning, Queen.

Reflection

How can you add some joy to your day?

29
APRIL

God doesn't take a long time to bless us, Queen.

We often take a long time to trust.

Reflection

What's holding up your progress?

30
APRIL

The attitude you hold
when you make a mistake or lose,
will dictate the length of time
until your next success, Queen.

Reflection

Are you ready to push until you birth your dreams?

MAY

01
MAY

Today's pursuits are tomorrow's wealth.

Make sure your efforts are invested in valuable actions, Queen.

Reflection

Does your task list for this week align with your future goals?

02
MAY

Remember, Queen: assets put money in your pocket
and liabilities take from you.

Lessen the liabilities.

Reflection

What are your assets? (Take 20 minutes today to
work on a strategy to increase them.)

03
MAY

Comparison is a confidence killer, Queen.

Never compare.

Reflection

What do you love most about yourself?

04
MAY

Praise is power, Queen.

Make it a point to recognize and acknowledge the good deeds of others.

Reflection

Has someone done something good for you recently?
Have you acknowledged them?

05
MAY

Be willing to try, Queen.

Be open to learning.

Reflection

Are you willing to make room in your schedule for
personal growth and experimentation?

06
MAY

Do one new and uncomfortable thing today, Queen.

It's time to grow.

Reflection

How do you feel about switching things up?

07
MAY

Words are powerful, Queen.

Use them to speak highly of yourself and uplift others.

No complaining allowed.

Reflection

Are you mindful of your conversations?

08
MAY

Confidence today, Queen.

Exude confidence.

Reflection

How's your posture?
Are you walking in your power or fear?

09
MAY

Meditate, Queen.
Sit in silence and breathe.
If you're alive it means God's not done with you yet.

Reflection

Are you comfortable in silence?

10
MAY

Instead of giving yourself reasons why something
won't work, come up with all the ways that it will.
Don't live in your head.
Go for it, Queen.

Reflection

List three reasons why things will work out for you
today?

11
MAY

Leave people, places and things better off than you
found them, Queen.

That is the true essence of royalty.

Reflection

How do you think people feel after spending time
with you?

12
MAY

Continue to have people be in awe of your beautiful heart, Queen.

Always give or do more than expected.

Reflection

How can you be extra today?

13
MAY

Excuses do just that. They excuse you from reaching your highest potential and attaining goals.

Don't offer any more excuses.

Queens provide results only.

Reflection

What are some results you're looking forward to?

14
MAY

Love overcomes fear every time, Queen.

Love <u>always</u> wins.

Reflection

How can you overcome fear with love today?

15
MAY

Pause, Queen.

Take a break from your concerns and enjoy
the present moment.

It truly is a gift.

Reflection

Take a mindful minute. Write down how you are
feeling in this very moment.

16
MAY

To achieve something extraordinary,
follow these steps:

- <u>BE</u>: Reflect on the qualities you need to embody to sustain what you desire (write them down).
- <u>DO</u>: Identify what is required to bring your vision to life (take action).
- <u>HAVE</u>: Clearly define what you want to achieve (focus solely on that outcome).

Be. Do. Have, Queen.

Reflection

Are you genuinely prepared to <u>become </u>the person you need to be to progress?

17
MAY

Move in silence.

Always let your success do the talking, Queen.

Reflection

What is your definition of success?

18
MAY

Have fun, Queen.

Life is short but it doesn't have to be boring.

Reflection

When was the last time you had a really good time?
Can you recreate the experience or top it?

19
MAY

Be a source of positive energy, not a drain, Queen.

Stay in tune with yourself and recognize the difference in how others impact your energy as well.

Reflection

How can you be more uplifting today?

20
MAY

Today, decide to have a great day (no matter what).
Then, go ahead and make it a great day, Queen.

No exceptions.

Reflection

How does it feel to make up your mind?

21
MAY

Brighten a stranger's day with a compliment and notice the ripple effect of your gesture, Queen.

Reflection

Did you make someone feel important today?
How did that make you feel?

22
MAY

Practice the art of non-attachment.

Allow what arrives to enter, and what departs to leave.

Do this as often as possible, Queen.

Reflection

Just for today, can you let go of expectations?

23
MAY

Make yourself a priority, Queen.

Get in the habit of scheduling "self-check-ins".

Reflection

Where are you on your priority list?

24
MAY

Occasionally, time can outwit us; therefore, act on what must be accomplished today, Queen.

No more waiting.

Reflection

What systems can you put in place to overcome the fear of action?

25
MAY

You are healing generations through your self-love,
Queen.

I am proud of you.

Reflection

Do you realize that YOU are the answer to your
ancestors' prayers?

26
MAY

Keep your standards, Queen.

Don't waiver.

Let the world rise to meet you <u>exactly</u> where you are.

Reflection

Write a list of your deal breakers for people, places and things. Then, adhere to them.

27
MAY

Queen, little things can add up to big things.

So, do not let the little things go.

Reflection

Are you comfortable addressing issues directly?

28
MAY

Acknowledgement is a major step toward healing, Queen.

State your truth.

Reflection

What is something you need to be honest with yourself about?

29
MAY

Even in discomfort, sit with your feelings, Queen.
They are trying to tell you something.

PAIN = Pay. Attention. Inwards. Now.

Reflection

What are some healthy ways you can process your
emotions?

30
MAY

Your past does not have to dictate your future, Queen.

Be the reason others hold on to hope.

Reflection

Do you have a testimony to share?

31
MAY

As you live abundantly, you unconsciously give others
permission to do the same.

Let your lifestyle speak, Queen.

Reflection

Does your life reflect an abundant mindset
or scarcity?

JUNE

01
JUNE

Be slow to anger, Queen.

Everyone is doing the best they can at any given moment.

Remember this often.

Reflection

Who can you forgive today?

02

JUNE

You're required to be your best, not perfect.

Give yourself permission to make mistakes, Queen.

Reflection

Write a list of 10 things you've learned through making mistakes. Then, share your learning lessons with someone you love.

03

JUNE

Experiencing you in this lifetime is an honor, Queen.

An absolute privilege.

Reflection

Affirm: "My presence is supreme. I am a gift."

04
JUNE

There is so much the world has to offer you, Queen.

Don't choose anything mediocre.

Go big.

Reflection

Affirm: "I am worthy of the best."

05
JUNE

Certain connections last for a specific period, serve a
particular purpose, or endure a lifetime.

Recognizing the nature of each
can guide you in understanding
when to release them gracefully, Queen.

Reflection

In your journal, list seven things that you are
releasing. Then, list seven replacements that will
enrich your life with beauty and positivity.

06
JUNE

For the next 24 hours, be intentional about what you say.

Say something nice or nothing at all, Queen.

Reflection

Is speaking kindly a habit for you?

07
JUNE

Create a confidence journal.

Record affirmations and reminders that bolster your self-esteem.

Review entries regularly, Queen, (especially when you need a reminder of how amazing you are).

Reflection

Self-promotion is key; if you don't do it, who else will?

08

JUNE

There is nothing wrong with you, Queen.

Great things take time.

YOUR great thing is on its way!

Reflection

What can you do <u>now</u> to prepare for your miracle?

09
JUNE

Make room for fresh beginnings, Queen.

Your new season is about to start.

Reflection

What fresh start are you manifesting?

10

JUNE

Learn to take mixed signals and inconsistency as a no.

Decline any further participation, Queen.

Reflection

Did you know that a person's actions (not words)
will always tell you exactly how they feel about you?

11
JUNE

Put the phone down for one hour every day and engage in an outside activity, Queen.

Let nature talk to you.

Reflection

When's the last time you went on a walking meditation?

12
JUNE

Your "best day" can be today, Queen.

You're one thought away.

Reflection

Describe your ideal day. How does it start? What are you doing?

13
JUNE

Be a problem-solver.

Success involves overcoming challenges, Queen,
not avoiding them.

Reflection

What's a new way to look at a troubling situation?

14
JUNE

Don't get impatient when things take too long, Queen.

Not now doesn't mean never.

Reflection

Would you consider yourself a patient person?

15
JUNE

Let today be easy, Queen.

Practice being in the flow.

Reflection

Do you truly believe you are worthy of a life without struggle?

16
JUNE

Although often said, your life truly is a reflection of
your mindset.

To change your life, shift your thinking, Queen.

Reflection

What do your life situations reveal about your inner
thought process?

17
JUNE

Queen, prepare.

What you've been praying for is almost here.

Reflection

When opportunity knocks, will you be ready?

18
JUNE

Queen, remember: Psalm 37: 25

In other words, God is faithful and <u>everything</u> will be okay.

Reflection

Which scripture passage
do you find most comfort in?

19

JUNE

When you make a mistake or lose something, reassess and figure out what went wrong.

Don't blame luck.

Blaming luck never helped anyone reach their goals any faster, Queen.

Reflection

Are you willing to take ownership of your life?

20
JUNE

Focus on what matters, Queen.

Use your energy for where you're going, not where you've been.

Reflection

What have you been focusing on lately?

21
JUNE

How people treat you is a reflection of their beliefs, values and esteem.

How you treat others is how you feel about yourself.

Learn this and move accordingly, Queen.

Reflection

Are you treating others with love & kindness?

22

JUNE

"Now" is the magic word for success. "Tomorrow, next week, later and sometime" are all synonyms for failure.

Start <u>now</u>, Queen.

Reflection

Are you living urgently?

23

JUNE

Scrolling on the internet will only get you so far.

As a Queen, make sure to produce as much as you consume (if not more).

Reflection

What have you been creating lately?

24
JUNE

The world is waiting on you to step into your power.

Other lives are tied to your destiny, Queen.

Reflection

Affirm: "My purpose is bigger than me."

25

JUNE

Continue to work on three things, Queen.

Your belief, faith and <u>audacity</u>.

These are the keys you need to transform your life.

Reflection

What extent of fearlessness do you possess?

26
JUNE

You are the quintessential woman, Queen.

Own this.

Embody it and never forget.

Reflection

Play "I'm every woman" by Whitney Houston and sing it out LOUD!

27
JUNE

Queen, perfection is not a prerequisite to speak.
It's the willingness to be authentic and share your
thoughts that truly matters.

Reflection

Have you been holding back?
What do you have to say?

28
JUNE

Sometimes saying sorry is the beginning of a fresh start, Queen.

And sometimes forgiveness is the blessing.

Reflection

Would you be willing to embrace a new chapter?

29
JUNE

Someone is about to give up and needs to hear your story to go on, Queen.

There's power in your voice,
but it's up to you to use it.

Reflection

Will you share your story?

30
JUNE

Love is often expressed in unexpected forms, Queen.

Welcome them all.

Reflection

Do something for yourself or surprise another, in the name of love.

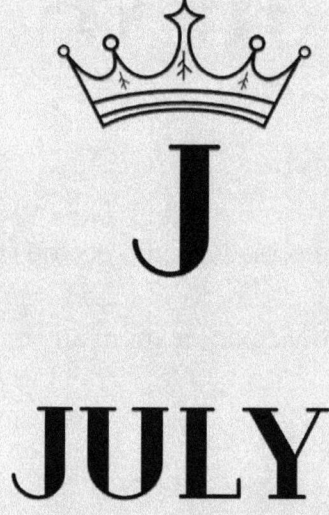

JULY

01
JULY

Appreciate nothing and gain even less.

Appreciate a bit, and abundance will surely follow, Queen.

Reflection

What are you thankful for?

02

JULY

Every big accomplishment is a series of little accomplishments, Queen.

Celebrate your small wins.

Reflection

Affirm: "One step at a time."

03
JULY

F.A.I.L= First Attempt In Learning

So, if you've ever "failed", congratulations on learning what doesn't work.

Cheers for trying something new, Queen!

Reflection

How do you feel when you F.A.I.L?

04
JULY

Courage can show up as tears.
Strength can look like going to bed and saying,
"I'll try again tomorrow."
And wisdom can be asking for help, Queen.

Reflection

Which virtue do you need to use today?

05
JULY

Look in the mirror and repeat:

"I love you, Queen. You are my best friend and there isn't anything you can do to change my mind.
I love you."

Reflection

When's the last time you gave yourself a hug?

06
JULY

Proverbs 3:5

Give up the need to understand everything, Queen.

Reflection

Are you willing to trust today?

07

JULY

Study yourself, Queen.

Reflection

What do you value most about who you are?

08
JULY

Trust your instincts, Queen.

If something doesn't sit well with you,
it's worth a closer look.

Reflection

Do you evaluate how you feel prior to making big
decisions?

09
JULY

Embrace your curiosity, Queen.

Everything isn't always as it seems and questions can be the gateway to knowledge.

Reflection

With what frequency do you find yourself asking questions?

10
JULY

Today, let your presence be felt
without reservation, Queen.

You are royalty after all, aren't you?

Reflection

How comfortable are you with being seen?

11
JULY

Stand tall in your power, Queen.
The world may not always acknowledge your
regalness, but it is undeniable.

Reflection

Journal about the magnitude of who you are.

12
JULY

Embrace your worth, Queen.

There's no need for compromise.

Reflection

Do you want an ordinary life or a great one?

13
JULY

Are you striving for victory or merely avoiding defeat, Queen?

Both require energy just a <u>different</u> strategy.

Reflection

What's your mindset today?

14
JULY

In a world where all is possible, take a chance.

You never know when you might strike gold, Queen.

Reflection

When was the last time you took a leap of faith?

15
JULY

Develop a very good relationship with uncertainty.
Your comfort zone is the danger zone.
There is no growth there, Queen.

Reflection

What is your relationship like with the unknown?

16
JULY

Dear Queen, reminder:

You are worth loving.

You are worth saving.

Reflection

Do you believe you are worthy of unconditional love?

17
JULY

Queen, specificity breeds cooperation.

Get clear on your goals.

Reflection

What's the target?

18
JULY

In the words of Publius Syrus "a wise man will be master of his mind. A fool will be its slave."

Train your thoughts, Queen.

Reflection

What are you mastering?

19
JULY

Alone doesn't have to mean lonely, Queen.

There's beauty in solitude.

Reflection

Can you set aside 30 minutes every day to be alone
with yourself?

20
JULY

Combine persistence with experimentation.

See what sticks, Queen.

Reflection

Have you tried new ways to achieve your objective?

21
JULY

Create a voice memo of your personal pep talk.

Listen to it several times a day, Queen.

Reflection

How does it feel to be your own hype woman?

22
JULY

Dress up and take yourself out.

Buy yourself some beautiful flowers
(or whatever else you may like).

Treat yourself like the royal Queen you are
and let everyone else follow suit.

Reflection

When do you feel most like a Queen?

23
JULY

There is a lot of self-love in the word no, Queen.

Feel free to use your "no" often.

Reflection

What are some ways you express self-love?

24
JULY

Don't rush.

When in doubt, go at your own pace, Queen.

Reflection

Affirm: "Slow and steady.
I am taking my time today."

25

JULY

Look at you doing your best
and letting God take care of the rest.

You go, Queen!

Reflection

What's one small thing you can do today
to make yourself proud?

26
JULY

The world is big, Queen.

Explore it.

Remember to enjoy your one life.

Reflection

Where have you always wanted to go?

27
JULY

Embarking on a solo journey doesn't mean you'll walk alone forever.

Keep the faith and chase your dreams, Queen.

Soon you'll find yourself surrounded by endless supporters.

Reflection

Affirm: " I will attract the right people on my journey to success."

28
JULY

Queen, the people you know will influence your success or lack thereof.

Choose your circle wisely.

Reflection

Who's on your team?

29
JULY

It's our expectations, not reality, that let us down.

When we don't expect anything,
we can be grateful for everything, Queen.

Reflection

Dedicate a day to not expecting anything from
anyone.

30
JULY

Without taking chances, there are no gains.

No daring, no benefits.

No venture, no reward, Queen.

Reflection

Are you willing to take a chance?

31
JULY

When you're not true to yourself, you make it easier for others to be disloyal to you too, Queen.

Stay loyal.

Reflection

Are you committed to you?

A

AUGUST

01
AUGUST

Joy is not better than sorrow.

Every emotion has a message for us, Queen.

All feelings serve a purpose.

Reflection

How are you <u>feeling</u> today?

02
AUGUST

Queen, each season has value.

Know and understand the time you're in:
planting, harvesting, or reaping.

Reflection

Which season of life are you in?

03
AUGUST

The distance between where you are and where you want to go is confidence, Queen.

Boost up your confidence.

Reflection

Have you been repeating your affirmations ?

04
AUGUST

Grief comes and goes.
Be gentle with yourself when recovering.
You're doing the best you can, Queen.

Reflection

What are you healing from?

05
AUGUST

Lighten up.

Don't take life so seriously, Queen.

Reflection

What's your favorite life motto?

06
AUGUST

Notice what activity you're doing and who's with you when you feel happiest.

Recreate the experience as often as possible, Queen.

Reflection

Who always puts a smile on your face?
Can you talk to them today?

07
AUGUST

You can't fix a problem with the same level of thinking that created it, Queen.

Think higher.

Reflection

Is it time to take a step back?

08
AUGUST

Someone might be observing you when you least expect it, Queen.

Stay poised and well-positioned at all times.

Reflection

What do you do to activate "Queen Mode"?

09
AUGUST

To stay in your feminine energy, slow down.

Take your time, Queen.

Reflection

Why such a rush?

10
AUGUST

Music is healing.

Soothe yourself with beautiful music today, Queen.

Reflection

What's your favorite uplifting song?

11
AUGUST

Turn your pain into purpose, Queen.

Apply what you've learned and create a better life.

Reflection

Read or re-read the book "The Alchemist" by Paulo Coelho.

12
AUGUST

Being broke is hard. Being rich is hard.

Being fit is hard. Being overweight is hard.

Choose your hard, Queen.

Reflection

Have you been keeping up with your self-discipline?

13

AUGUST

Treat your body with love and respect, Queen.

You only get one.

Reflection

Is your body well-cared for, like the sacred place that it is?

14
AUGUST

Let go of the past, Queen.

If something didn't work out, it was for a reason.

Reflection

Do your thoughts tend to focus more on the past or
the present?

15
AUGUST

Cry if you must but never go back to what broke you,
Queen.

<u>Never</u>.

Reflection

How does it feel to be victorious?

16
AUGUST

Breaks are essential, Queen—take them,
but don't linger too long.

Keep going.

Reflection

Do you need a break?

17
AUGUST

The sun remains lovely after all this time.

Enjoy it when you can, Queen.

Reflection

What's your favorite outdoor activity?
Add it to your agenda this week.

18
AUGUST

Use your inner wisdom.

All solutions reside within you, Queen.

Reflection

What's been on your heart lately?

19
AUGUST

Knowledge of your history
can inform your direction.

Find out about where you came from, Queen.

Reflection

Who are your ancestors?

20
AUGUST

Start collaborating more.
No woman is an island.
You need people and they need you, Queen.

Reflection

How can you improve your teamwork skills?

21
AUGUST

You are your own greatest love, Queen.

You are "the one."

Reflection

What can you do to celebrate yourself today?

22
AUGUST

Help whenever you can.

Contribute when you have a lot.
Share when you have little.

It will all come full-circle.

All your good will come back to you, Queen.

Reflection

When's the last time you gave back?

23
AUGUST

Projecting confidence often starts with your appearance.

Dress with intention.

Elevate your brand, Queen.

Reflection

How can you upgrade your style?

24
AUGUST

Learn to communicate effectively
(even when you are upset).

Always maintain your grown woman vibes, Queen.

Reflection

In what ways are you improving your communication
skills?

25

AUGUST

Keep people around that validate you.

You start to heal when you feel seen and heard,
Queen.

Reflection

Do the people around "see" you?

26
AUGUST

You are unique and irreplaceable, Queen.

Without you, the world would not be the same.
Your presence makes all the difference.

YOU MATTER.

Reflection

Affirm: "I matter."

27

AUGUST

You get to take up space, Queen.

Shrink for no one.

Reflection

Have you been standing on business when it comes
to you?

28
AUGUST

Arrange an informational interview with someone
who holds the position you aspire to.

Having a great mentor
can simplify the journey through life, Queen.

Reflection

Who are you learning from?

29
AUGUST

Express your self-respect through your speech, attire, and behavior, Queen.

While being "cute" has its appeal, gaining respect is of greater value.

Reflection

Are you demonstrating self-respect?

30
AUGUST

People respect what you have to say.
Choose your words wisely, Queen.
You have more influence than you know.

Reflection

Are you leveraging your impact positively?

31
AUGUST

You can't have big dreams with low self-esteem.
Keep nurturing your self-assurance.
You've got this, Queen.

Reflection

What makes you feel like superwoman?

SEPTEMBER

01
SEPTEMBER

Love always surrounds you, Queen.

Pay attention.

Reflection

Initiate a heartfelt conversation about the meaning of love with someone important to you and learn about their view. What does being loved look like for them? What does it look like for you?

02
SEPTEMBER

Although it doesn't always seem like it, some aspects of your life are an answer to one of your prayers.

Honor that today, Queen.

Reflection

What are some positive changes that have happened since this time last year?

03
SEPTEMBER

Read about the "Law of Correspondence".

Your inner world will always mirror your outer.

Therefore, allow self-kindness to lead you to a kinder world, Queen.

Reflection

Do you know the laws of the universe?

04
SEPTEMBER

Advancing to higher levels requires the willingness to leave your current level behind, Queen.

Reflection

What are you willing to give up for your new life?

05
SEPTEMBER

Success requires heart and soul effort.

Only commit to what you truly desire.

Anything else would just be a waste of time, Queen.

Reflection

What are you dedicated to?

06
SEPTEMBER

Today, let's make a conscious decision to address our problems directly.

No more dismissing or mislabeling.

Feel it and heal it, Queen.

Reflection

Can you sit in discomfort without numbing?

07
SEPTEMBER

Travel solo, Queen. At least once in your life.

There is something outside of your city and state that you need to see.

Reflection

Where would you go on a solo trip?

08
SEPTEMBER

Focus on the present moment, Queen.

You are <u>exactly</u> where you need to be.

Reflection

Can you accept where you are now?

09
SEPTEMBER

Darling, you are a Queen.
And once you know what that truly means.
I pray for anyone or anything that tries to stop you.

Reflection

Affirm: "I am Queen."

10
SEPTEMBER

Perception vs. reality.

How we see things isn't always how they are, Queen.

Reflection

What are the facts of your life?

11
SEPTEMBER

Don't be so afraid to get it wrong
that you don't try, Queen.

Trust your gut.

Reflection

When's the last time you took a chance?

12
SEPTEMBER

Who you are and what you do are <u>not</u> the same,
Queen.

Your worth is internal.

Reflection

How would you describe yourself, setting aside your
professional and social labels?

13
SEPTEMBER

May today be your best day yet, Queen.
May your goings and comings be covered and blessed.
May miracles happen for you, back-to-back.
And may you have a renewed spirit and mind.

Reflection

Did you know that all things were working out in
your favor?

14
SEPTEMBER

Silence often goes unrewarded.
Declare your desires, Queen.
Claim them (since they are yours).
Then, prepare to receive them.

Reflection

Write a list of everything you want God to take care
of this month. Then, consider them done.

15
SEPTEMBER

Instead of saying "I want..", try saying
"I'm preparing for..."
And monitor the energy shift, Queen.

Reflection

Are you paying attention to your language?

16
SEPTEMBER

Another Queen's beauty & amazingness is simply a reflection of yours.

Don't be jealous and don't tear another woman down.

Honor all Queens.

Reflection

Do you ever get jealous? If so, why?

17
SEPTEMBER

Let your boundaries be stronger than your emotions.
If you settle for less, you will always get less than what
you settled for, Queen.

Reflection

Affirm: "No low-quality experiences shall be
allowed."

18
SEPTEMBER

Speak to the woman you aspire to be.

Call the Queen inside of you forward.

Reflection

Who's leading you right now,
is it the strongest version of yourself ?

19
SEPTEMBER

Exercise, Queen.
You have only one body.
Take care of it.

Reflection

What's your definition of a "good" workout?

20
SEPTEMBER

You are the breakthrough you're waiting on, Queen.

Reflection

Are you capitalizing on your abilities?

21
SEPTEMBER

Make your moves, Queen.

The right people will always show up.

Reflection

Are you willing to stop postponing happiness?

22
SEPTEMBER

Your qualifications exceed the norm, Queen.

Your humility is impressive.

Reflection

Which tasks do you perform with ease?

23

SEPTEMBER

Do not spin the block.
I repeat: DO NOT spin the block.
If you left something or someone alone,
it was for a reason, Queen.
Trust yourself.

Reflection

When someone shows you who they are,
do you believe them?

24
SEPTEMBER

Good health is the real wealth.

Prioritize your inner Queen.

Reflection

What's a healthy habit you can commit to for the
rest of the month?

25
SEPTEMBER

Fear will cause you to stop reaching for things, which are already yours.

NO FEAR, QUEEN.

Reflection

Write the phrase "I am unstoppable", ten times.
Then, affirm the statement out loud ten times
(and say it like you mean it).

26
SEPTEMBER

Who you were and who you are now can be two
different people, Queen.

As you evolve, make peace with this
and the world will too.

Reflection

Who are you <u>now</u>?

27
SEPTEMBER

Seeking connection is a beautiful desire, but it should not be the sole reason to remain in unsatisfactory relationships.

You are worthy of relationships that are fulfilling and enriching, Queen.

You are worthy of real love.

Reflection

What's your definition of a "healthy relationship"? Have you ever witnessed one?

28

SEPTEMBER

Emotional Intelligence, Queen.
Learn your attachment style so you can stop confusing
anxiety and obsession with love.

Reflection

Are you secure, avoidant or anxious?

29
SEPTEMBER

In the words of Virginia Woolf,
"No need to hurry. No need to sparkle.
No need to be anybody else but yourself."

Be yourself today, Queen.

Reflection

What does authenticity mean to you?

30
SEPTEMBER

Results or excuses, Queen.

Your actions will decide today.

Reflection

In your environment, are people more likely to talk
about their accomplishments, or do they tend to
explain why things weren't done?

OCTOBER

01
OCTOBER

You are wiser than any distraction, Queen.

You are tougher than any obstacle.

Reflection

When was the last time you acknowledged your
ability to handle challenges?

02
OCTOBER

Embrace the belief that the world is rooting for you
because they are, Queen.

Reflection

Are you willing to believe that life is on your side?

03
OCTOBER

As William Henley stated,
"You are the master of your fate.
You are the captain of your soul."
The power to shape your future and fulfill your
desires rests with you, Queen.
No one else.

Reflection

What would it take to increase your self-belief?

04
OCTOBER

Whatever you want is within reach, Queen.

It's probably closer than you think.

Reflection

Today, for 17 seconds or more, meditate on your desired outcome. Then, show gratitude (count it as done).

05
OCTOBER

Accept people for who they are, Queen.
However, be true to who you are and what you want.
Don't waste energy trying to fix or convince others
(it never works).

Reflection

Are you willing to keep things simple today?

06
OCTOBER

If the right people show up in life, great.

If not, great.

Fall in love with you, Queen.

Reflection

Could it be that you are your own best friend?

07
OCTOBER

Be nice today, Queen,
even when others are not as nice to you.

Reflection

Can you commit to brightening
at least one person's day, today?

08
OCTOBER

Don't allow the world to hold you to unrealistic standards, Queen.

You are allowed to be imperfect.

Reflection

Whose standards are you following—yours or the world's?

09
OCTOBER

Queen, here's how you can tell if someone is an asset
in your life:
Pay attention to how you feel during
and after your interactions.
Do they leave you feeling uplifted or drained?

That's your answer.

Reflection

Does your tribe match your vibe?

10
OCTOBER

Raise your price, Queen—both in business
and in your personal life.

Only those who bring value should have access to
you.

Reflection

Do you truly value your time?

11
OCTOBER

You are an inspiration, Queen.
Someone needs to hear <u>your</u> specific voice, writing,
thoughts and views.
The timing will never be "perfect" and you will never
be 100% ready.
Share your gifts and talent anyway.

Reflection

Are you willing to let your light shine?

12
OCTOBER

All is well, Queen.

All is well.

Reflection

Describe your perfect day in detail.
Then, make it happen.

13
OCTOBER

True faith is about believing in a higher power,
no matter what unfolds.

Focus on your faith and not just the outcome, Queen.

Reflection

Where have you placed your faith?

14
OCTOBER

Be kind to yourself, Queen,
and tolerate only kindness from others.

Reflection

What aspect of your personality do you value the
most?

15
OCTOBER

The financial freedom you desire may require an upfront investment, Queen.

Be prepared to sacrifice a little now for something greater later.

Reflection

What will you do differently to attain the type of lifestyle you want?

16
OCTOBER

When one door closes another door opens.
This often leads to an unexpected
yet beautiful beginning.

Don't spend too much time focusing on closed doors,
Queen.

(Also, to be honest, the entire building is yours
anyway.)

Reflection

How do you feel about redirection?

17
OCTOBER

You have the power to reinvent yourself, Queen.
Start over as many times as it takes—each time will be
better than the last.

Reflection

Affirm: "There is no limit to God's grace."

18
OCTOBER

Don't fear losing people, Queen.

Fear losing yourself chasing approval.

Reflection

Have you verified yourself?

19
OCTOBER

Distractions prolong greatness, Queen.
Make sure your life is in order.
Social media and fun engagements can wait.

Reflection

Do your actions reflect your priorities?

20
OCTOBER

You get to be the hero of your own story, Queen.

You must first decide.

Reflection

Write a letter to your inner child.
Let her know you've got everything under control.

21
OCTOBER

When your instincts signal that something isn't right,
heed the feeling.

Always have confidence in your intuition.

After all, you possess royal discernment, Queen.

Reflection

How do you know when
your intuition is speaking vs. trauma?

22
OCTOBER

Read the poem "My Wage" by Jessie B. Rittenhouse
and tape it to your wall.
You're not asking for too much, Queen.
Whatever wage you demand of life,
it will gladly pay.

Reflection

What's your definition of "a lot"?

23
OCTOBER

Read up on a new topic today, Queen.

Learn something new.

Reflection

Does the world strike you
as a place of adventure or dullness?

24
OCTOBER

Generational curses are real
but so is generational wisdom, Queen.

Reflection

Ask your mom or elder about the most challenging or
frightening experience they've ever encountered.

Observe if their story has had an impact or strikes a
chord with you.

25
OCTOBER

Run with lions, Queen.

Level up.

Reflection

Who's on your A-Team? Who are they "being" and what are they doing to make the world a better place?

26
OCTOBER

Choose people who choose you, Queen.
It may seem repetitive but you'll save yourself a lot of
wasted time and energy with this one simple rule.

Reflection

What are your thoughts on reciprocity?

27
OCTOBER

No one has to lose, Queen.
True Queens believe in creating win-win situations.
Find a way to make it work.

Reflection

Maintain a mindset that always asks "how can I
create a solution that works for everyone involved?"

28
OCTOBER

Don't speak meaninglessly, Queen.
Your words will start to hold less weight.
Consider your impact.
Silence is power.

Reflection

Do you believe you have the self-control to think
before you speak?

29
OCTOBER

Good friends are precious, Queen.

Cherish them.

Reflection

How can you demonstrate thankfulness to your friends?

30

OCTOBER

Hold yourself accountable, Queen.

A stumble doesn't mean you have to fall.

Reflection

Are you willing to get back on track or intensify your
efforts?

31
OCTOBER

You are one with the Creator,
a natural giver of life.

Breathe life into your dreams, goals and visions,
Queen.

Most importantly, pour life into yourself.

Reflection

Affirm out loud: "I am one with the Creator.
I am one with the Most High."

NOVEMBER

01

NOVEMBER

What if everything works out, Queen?

Reflection

Are you in control of your thoughts or are they
controlling you?

02

NOVEMBER

Big Dreams. Big Thoughts. Big Conversations.

Nothing little about you, Queen.

Reflection

What bold vision are you daring to believe in?

03
NOVEMBER

When things get difficult, push through the anxiety, fear, uncertainty and sadness.

Your miracle awaits you on the other side.

Push, Queen.

Reflection

What motivates you to stay determined?

04
NOVEMBER

There is no one more deserving of your genuine love, kindness and affection than you, Queen.

Reflection

Affirm: "I am the love that I'm looking for."

05
NOVEMBER

"A wise person will always find a way"
-Tanzanian proverb.

Find a way, Queen or create one.

Reflection

How can you do things the "Queen" way?

06

NOVEMBER

Starting your journey later in life is far better than
never starting at all, Queen.
You are the exception.
Go for it.

Reflection

What have you always wanted to do?

07

NOVEMBER

People can't read minds.
When something upsets you, make your feelings
known and make them clear, Queen.

Reflection

Do you need to take a class on effective
communication?

08
NOVEMBER

What is important to you is important, Queen.

Reflection

Create a list of what truly matters to you, and assess whether your daily activities align with it.

09
NOVEMBER

Choose to forgive, even in the absence of an apology.

Free yourself, Queen.

Reflection

Is there anyone or anything you need to forgive?
Would you be willing to do it today?

10
NOVEMBER

Refocus. Get back in the gym. Start a new hobby.
Don't wait until the new year starts.
Begin right where you stand, using whatever resources
you possess.
Start <u>today</u>, Queen.

Reflection

Are you running life or is life running you?

11

NOVEMBER

Make a wish, Queen.
Then graciously watch it unfold
(without your intervention).

Reflection

When was the last time you talked to God and when
was the last time you listened?

12
NOVEMBER

The difference between ordinary and extraordinary is
the extra, Queen.

Be extra today.

Reflection

How differently would you live if you were not
afraid of judgement or failure?

13

NOVEMBER

With the right company,
just being yourself is enough, Queen.

Reflection

Do you feel like you're being your authentic self in all
aspects of life? If no, why not?

14
NOVEMBER

Give life 100%.

Life will certainly return the favor, Queen.

Reflection

Can you put a number on your effort lately?
What is the percentage?

15
NOVEMBER

We all have a peak time when we're most productive during the day.

Use these high-energy periods for your most important tasks, Queen.

Reflection

Are you working smarter or harder?

16
NOVEMBER

You are God's favorite.
God wanted you in this world, at this particular time.

Walk with your head held high
knowing that God is pleased with you, Queen.

Reflection

Affirm: "I am God's Favorite."

17
NOVEMBER

Be mindful of how you view yourself.

Self-perception can either push you forward or hold you back, Queen.

Reflection

How do you think others view you?
How do you see yourself?

18
NOVEMBER

On the days you feel insecure or uncertain about the future, do this:

- Give yourself a hug for ten seconds
- Kiss the back of your right hand
- Use your right hand to touch your heart for two seconds
- Repeat out loud: "Thank you Queen, for doing the best you can."

Reflection

Consider leaving yourself sticky notes on the wall or mirror, fill your space with positive reminders.

19
NOVEMBER

You don't have to be perfect to give advice
or coach others.

If you've been through something and endured.

You are eligible to lead someone else, Queen.

Reflection

Who are you leading?

20
NOVEMBER

Pain typically goes away
when you have learned the lesson, Queen.

Reflection

What is a valuable lesson you've learned during the
month of November?

21
NOVEMBER

Failure doesn't mean forget it, Queen.

Find a different approach.

Reflection

How do you perceive failure?

22
NOVEMBER

Proactively present a solution in the workplace
without being asked.

Be an asset, Queen.

Reflection

Do you like what you do for work (enough) to make
a difference?

23
NOVEMBER

No matter how good you may treat others,
they may not be good to you, Queen.

Be good anyway.

Reflection

Write a list of everything you're releasing today.
Then, stop keeping score.

24
NOVEMBER

Put yourself in another Queen's shoes.

Grant people the same grace you would wish to receive, Queen.

Reflection

What are your thoughts on compassion?
Is this something you are able to give?

25

NOVEMBER

When your desire for transformation is greater than
your desire for the familiar,
change becomes inevitable, Queen.

Reflection

Are you really ready for life to be different?

26
NOVEMBER

If something affects one, it affects us all.

We are all connected, Queen.

Reflection

Recall an instance when another person's issue also became a challenge for you. How did this make you feel?

27
NOVEMBER

A beautiful friend once reminded me,
"the Queen is the most powerful player on the chess
board."

Never forget your power, Queen.

Reflection

How would you live differently if you were to act
from a place of power today?

28

NOVEMBER

Individuals with merely a fraction of your abilities are
living lavishly by simply taking a leap.
Stop doubting your capabilities and take action.
You will figure things out as you go, Queen.
(Don't you always?)

Reflection

Why do you think you're not ready? Are you
underestimating your ability to learn during the
process?

29

NOVEMBER

Make sure your actions are indicative of your top priorities, Queen.

No more procrastinating.

Reflection

Can you identify the highest priority in your life at the moment?

30
NOVEMBER

If you can read this, you are blessed Queen,
more than you realize.

Reflection

Close your eyes and answer, "what are you grateful
for in this moment?"

DECEMBER

01
DECEMBER

Don't say no to yourself before the world has had a chance to support you.

Don't sell yourself short, Queen.

Reflection

What feelings come up when you think about clearly asking for what you truly want?

02
DECEMBER

The minds of the diligent are always on positive outcomes.

Be an observer of your thoughts today, Queen.

Reflection

What do you find yourself constantly thinking about and is it serving you?

03

DECEMBER

What you resist, persists, Queen.

Reflection

Sit alone in silence for 10 minutes. Journal about how you truly feel and what you need at this moment.

04
DECEMBER

Do what you need to do for this moment, Queen.

Cross the bridge when you get there.

Reflection

How does overthinking support you?
How does it not?

05

DECEMBER

Make it a point to be honest & vulnerable for the next 24hrs.

More Transparency > Less Hiding

It's time to be seen, Queen.

Reflection

How does it feel to be recognized?

06

DECEMBER

Consider who is making the choices in your life:
the adult Queen or the wounded inner child.

After introspection, let the adult Queen take over.

Reflection

Are you being driven by past traumas or self-love?

07

DECEMBER

A mindset is holding you back
from operating at your full potential.

Once you identify it,
you'll become unstoppable, Queen.

Reflection

Journal about why you haven't accomplished
your goals yet.

Is it a lack of confidence or simply disinterest?

08

DECEMBER

Contrary to what society may preach,
there's always more, Queen.
More love.
More joy.
More excitement.
More life.
Always.

Reflection

How does it feel to expect miracles rather than
struggle?

09

DECEMBER

Instead of giving excuses, try saying
"this is not a priority for me".

If you don't like the sound of that,
no more excuses, Queen.

Reflection

Challenge yourself to make no excuses for the next
24 hours.

10
DECEMBER

"Gye Nyame," a cherished expression in Ghana,
represents the influence of God.
When spirits are low, it's <u>God</u> who uplifts.
In moments of fear, it's <u>God</u> who provides courage.
At the crossroads of uncertainty, it's <u>God</u> who guides.
<u>God</u> is above all, Queen.
Remember this truth today.

"Gye Nyame."

Reflection

Create a list in your journal of moments when you've
witnessed divine intervention, either in your life or
others. Refer to it when needed.

11
DECEMBER

No matter the struggle,
another Queen has dealt with it or is facing it too.

You are not alone.

Reflection

Do you believe you must face certain challenges
alone? If so, is this supporting or hindering you?

12
DECEMBER

Networking brings blessings, Queen.

The people you know and the places you go will help you reach your goals.

Stay open to the amazing opportunities that await you.

Reflection

Who or what are you connected to? Tap in.

13
DECEMBER

Learn to be okay with looking foolish, Queen.
It's in those moments that you'll discover what it truly
means to be a winner.

Reflection

Do you really want to win or do you want to look
good (while losing)?

14
DECEMBER

Don't be in such a rush to have a great life
that you miss a good one.
Have goals.
Have dreams.
Also, pause to have some tea,
or whatever else makes you happy, Queen.

Reflection

How does it feel to just breathe?

15
DECEMBER

When you break a habit, make sure to replace it with something beneficial.

Set yourself up for success, Queen.

Reflection

Make a list of your vices and next to them, write its healthy replacement. Create a plan. Then, stick to it.

16
DECEMBER

Whatever you are consuming
will soon be consuming you, Queen.
Be <u>very</u> selective about what you ingest.
This includes people, places and things.

Reflection

What are the side effects of what you are listening
to, seeing and eating? Is it making you a better version
of yourself or worse?

17
DECEMBER

Real growth often involves the process of
unlearning and eliminating, Queen.

Be open to reevaluating what you consider to be true.

Reflection

What were some values instilled in you during your
early years and how have they influenced your
current identity?

18
DECEMBER

Half of the time the people you may view as competition are losing.

Focus on your race, Queen.

Reflection

What are some practical steps you can take to avoid comparison?

19
DECEMBER

Self-awareness can be a lifetime process, Queen.

Make it a beautiful one.

Reflection

How is your evolution going? What can you do to
make the journey more pleasurable?

20
DECEMBER

Just as others have realized their dreams,
you too possess this power, Queen.
Nothing is "too good" for you.
Expect the best because that's exactly what you are.
You are simply the best.

Reflection

List three outcomes are you looking forward to.
Write them in present tense, starting with "I am so
happy and grateful that...". Then, witness the magic
as it manifests.

21
DECEMBER

If you want to pass a test,
you must give up distractions and study.
Should you want an amazing physique,
you must let go of poor habits and dedicate time to
clean eating and the gym.
Attaining a high standard of living
necessitates sacrifice, Queen.

Reflection

What are you willing to forgo, in order to have what
you say you want?

22
DECEMBER

Some endeavors may not be easy
but they can be worth it.
Don't overlook valuable opportunities simply because
they require a little extra effort, Queen.

It's the extra that make things worthwhile.

Reflection

What is one goal that scares you? Determine one
small action you can take today to progress towards
achieving that goal.

23

DECEMBER

Now is not the time to shrink, Queen.
However, only you get to make the choice.
Will you choose fear or faith?

Reflection

Are you ready to step into the spotlight?

24
DECEMBER

Before every blessing, there is a test.

Pass the test, Queen.

Reflection

What do you think life is trying to tell or teach you
during this chapter?

25

DECEMBER

The Divine is in you, Queen.

Success is inevitable.

Reflection

What's your definition of success? How will you
know when you've won?

26
DECEMBER

The impact you will make on others
far exceeds your fear.

Trust in the magic of who you are, Queen.

Get out of your own way.

Reflection

How can you remove the obstacles you've placed in
your own path?

27
DECEMBER

Anything truly destined for you won't leave, Queen.

Even when closure is absent, <u>persevere</u>.

Reflection

List the positive changes that have occurred this year after letting go of certain aspects and individuals from your life.

28
DECEMBER

Maybe what you thought you wanted, or were told to
want, isn't what you truly desire anymore
—and that's okay, Queen.

Things get to be different.

You have the right to want something different.

Reflection

What emotions come up for you when you think
about no longer wanting what you once desired?

29
DECEMBER

Mastery, Queen.

Ignore what society says—if it brings you joy, chase it.

Become a master of everything that fulfills you.

Reflection

What skill are you committed to perfecting in order
to earn the title of "great"?

30
DECEMBER

A devoted sister is a lifelong companion.

Cherish her presence, Queen.

She is truly one of life's greatest treasures.

Reflection

How has your sister (blood related or not) shaped
your life for the better?

31
DECEMBER

The next chapter of your life
is destined to be your greatest.

The victory is already within your grasp, Queen.

Step into it with confidence and embrace your royal
power —on the road to Queendom.

Reflection

How will your life look different this time next year?

BONUS

Loving you can be expensive, Queen,
but you're so very worth it.

Reflection

Did you know that I love and appreciate you for
being on this journey with me?

ACKNOWLEDGEMENTS

My First Published Book—Can You Believe It?!

I am beyond thrilled to share this moment with you! Heartfelt thanks to everyone who supported me through this writing journey. To those who offered inspiring words, sat with me, and helped bring this incredible book to life—I will forever cherish your support.

Though I penned these words, each message was divinely inspired. I hope this book serves you on your "Queendom" journey as it has for me.

Always remember: you are loved, you are beautiful and you are the best! I am immensely grateful to have a reader like you. Please pass this devotional on to another Queen who needs uplifting. Remember, hope is not a strategy—confidence is! Have a strategy of confidence and faith to succeed, knowing you can overcome any obstacle and achieve anything you set your mind to.

Thank you again for joining me on the wonderful and powerful Road to Queendom.

-Queen

About The Author

Queen S. Ofori is a captivating and multi-talented artist, Certified Life Coach, Human Resource and Career Consultant, holding a Master's Degree in Business Administration.

As a first-generation American born to Ghanaian parents, Queen's life is a testament to self-empowerment, spirituality, and creativity.

Driven by a passion to uplift women, Queen has successfully facilitated the "Road to Queendom" workshops, empowering participants to boost their self-esteem and seize better opportunities.

Queen lives by the principle of abundance and embraces life with a royal mindset, a belief she passionately shares through her words and actions.

(Photo taken by: Kofi Nyantakyi, NYC)

For business partnership, life or career coaching, and public speaking inquiries, please connect via:

Website: www.QueenOfori.com
Email: Support@QueenOfori.com
Instagram: @Official_QueenOfori
YouTube: @Official_QueenOfori
TikTok: @Official_QueenOfori
Facebook: Queen S. Ofori (Business Page)